Why
Not
Become
Fire?

Evelyn Mattern and Helen David Brancato

Why Not Become Fire?

ENCOUNTERS WITH WOMEN MYSTICS

ave maria press   Notre Dame, IN

© 1999 by Ave Maria Press, Inc.

International Standard Book Number: 0-87793-690-0

Cover and text design by Katherine Robinson Coleman.

Printed and bound in the United States of America.

Library of Congress Cataloging-in-Publication Data
Mattern, Evelyn.
      Why not become fire? : encounters with women mystics / Evelyn Mattern and Helen David Brancato.
             p.   cm.
    ISBN 0-87793-690-0
     1. Women mystics Poetry. 2. Christian poetry, American. 3. Women mystics Biography. 4. Mysticism Poetry. I. Brancato, Helen David.   II. Title.
PS3563.A8389W48 1999
809.1'9382—dc21
                                               99-30550
                                             CIP

To
the
Live Poets

Contents

The Eyes of Love

Who is the mystic? A mystic is one who has a direct experience of God and engages in a process of growing into and exploring it. Such direct experience may be unusual, but it is not something to be feared or avoided: the Psalmist, in fact, prays to see God face-to-face.

Mystics, we might say, can see God with the eyes of love. With such eyes—as Teresa of Avila would put it—the lover senses the presence of the beloved, even in the dark. In other words, the mystic is more than a visionary. Any number of stimulants can induce visions, but for the mystic, love is the only way. She may see so acutely that observers call her "crazy," but the wildness of her vision emanates from enhanced—not necessarily irrational—experience. Her intellect remains engaged.

Faith is engaged, as well. Despite the presence of evil in the world, the mystic believes that the universe is ultimately friendly. In her, what William James calls the "yes-function" finally prevails over the "no-function." We think of Etty Hillesum's leaps for joy as she walked inside the fence of the concentration camp. Julian of Norwich saw the world in God's palm as round as a ball, no bigger than a hazelnut, and said that it "lasts and always will because God loves it." Julian knew that "all shall be well, and all manner of things shall be well."

Because the mystic is in love, there arise in her unsuspected springs that can quench many thirsts and water improbable gardens. Through the action of prayer or the prayer of action, the mystic bursts out of her own ego and unleashes practical and creative efforts to share her love with the world. She is like the Boddhisattva in Buddhism, the figure who renounces enlightenment until all achieve it. She is like Catherine of Siena who—as the story goes—after her death stopped by a friend's house in Rome in order to prepare a meal. (Many women can believe that.)

Carol Lee Flinders (whose *Enduring Grace* has taught us much) points out that a woman mystic sometimes needs to claim "a room of her own." Teresa of Avila founded convents where the sisters could close the doors to their rooms. Catherine of Siena scalded herself so she could gain some independence from family members and their marriage plans for her. Emily Dickinson embraced the title "recluse." Dorothy Day left her bohemian friends to go study nursing on her own. A woman may need to claim her own life, fiercely at times, in order to give it to God.

Eventually, however, the mystic emerges from her room to work or to pray for murderers or missionaries or church reform or peace. Out of their solitude, mystics affirm and act on behalf of the universe. Indeed, the ultimate test of mysticism may be the willingness to emulate the *kenosis* of Jesus, his total giving or emptying on behalf of the world. Mechtild of Magdeburg describes God as a flood of love ("*minne-flut*") and as other molten and flowing elements. We remember that floods and molten lava rush not to vaulted heights but to the low places.

The Limits of Language

Mystics lament the inadequacy of words to express what they know. They seem to live by the Taoist adage, "Those who know, don't say; those who say, don't know," and hence they speak only under orders or on the authority of their love for others. Whether halting or eloquent, their language may be likened to music rather than conceptual speech. It is the language of poetry, which aims to express, rather than explain, experience. The mystic speaks of fire or wind or a feather on the breath of God; she does not elucidate a syllogism that logically deduces the existence of a First Cause. Even mystics who—like Edith Stein and Simone Weil—are profound practitioners of the rational, use imagery and analogy. Edith Stein speaks of meeting God in this way: "One can hear God knocking and yet not open. . . . Then one feels God's presence, but as something threatening, as a fetter." Simone Weil explains creation as "good broken up into pieces and scattered throughout evil." She compares the love of God to a stick chained to the hands of a blind-folded person: "this stick separates me from things, but I can explore them by means of it."

We find the same sort of language in the Psalms, the prophets, and in the sayings of Jesus himself. When Isaiah wishes to express Yahweh's pain because Israel has turned to idols, Yahweh says, "I groan like a woman in labor, I suffocate, I stifle" (42:14). Towards those ungrateful for their deliverance from slavery, Hosea has Yahweh complain, "Like a bear robbed of her cubs I will pounce on them, and tear the flesh around their hearts" (13:8).

Although they speak in images, mystics are theologians nonetheless; they simply take a more oblique approach to describing God than do rational theologians. Dom Sebastian Moore reminds us that the psalmist, for example, describes God as acting in ways that systematic theology wouldn't allow. Even Thomas Aquinas, the master of the analytic description of God and God's creation, alluded to the relative value of this more poetic approach. At the end, under the influence of his own experience of God, he declared that his careful, systematic work was "all straw."

Giving Birth

Just as artists give birth to music, painting, and poetry, mystics give birth to God in the world. They show us, rather than tell us, what God looks like. While Moses was receiving God's commandments all alone at the top of Mount Sinai, his sister Miriam was trying to get him to consider the possibility of governing the people in a more collegial manner. Mary Magdalen responded to Jesus' freeing her from demons by behaving like a free woman in an unfree environment. After Francis of Assisi's death and the capitulation of his order to ecclesiastical notions of poverty, Clare of Assisi kept alive the radical understanding and practice of poverty that they had shared. In a time of violence, Kateri Tekakwitha embraced a nonviolent way of life. The dimensions of God birthed by these women were often deemed untimely by others—as untimely, perhaps, as the birth in Bethlehem.

This Book as Process

We, writer and artist, sought to develop the poems and illustrations in this volume by emulating the mystic's way of tapping into her own unsuspected springs. Each poem emerged after the writer familiarized herself with the life and work of the mystic. Draft poems were put aside for awhile and looked at anew from the perspective of passed time and the artist's illustrations. Often the mystic's own words insinuated themselves into the poem (these are placed in quotation marks). More often, however, images or certain rhythms and lines echo the mystic's own speech or the speech her contemporaries might have used to tell her story.

This artist's process also emulates the mystic's. Using the methods of the Rorschach Test, which sometimes unearths what is embedded in the subconscious, she dropped india ink onto a wet surface. (A dry surface will not birth possibilities.) Then, stepping back to watch the ink bleed into the fluid surface, the artist relinquished control and allowed the medium to do the work. When the surface dried, she observed the results from a distance and with new eyes, open to the image that appeared.

The artist meditated, trying to focus on an image deep within the psyche. Never satisfied to look at the image from one direction only, she turned it again and again to discover further possibilities. Once the image had presented itself, certain shadows were deepened in order to lend greater prominence to the darkened form. As the shadows deepened, the lighter areas became brighter, stronger, more obvious. Drawing was kept to a minimum, so as not to lose the image given as a gift.

The entire process for pictures and poems constituted a form of meditation, with the presence of God found in the shadows. To this process poet and artist brought their experience of the mystic, and from it, they carried away an increased awareness of God and self in the world. The art form mirrored the growth of the soul, in which one creates in freedom and trust and—like the mystics, who "wait for God" in the darkness—does not fear the shadows.

Waiting Upon the Words

We recommend that the images in this book be approached by the reader in the way we approached them. Poetry, meant to be heard, should be read aloud, even memorized. It is concentrated language, to be spoken slowly, pondered. Words play off of other words, make images, link sounds. One does not read through poetry as one does not sprint through a museum. One waits upon the words, as upon visual images. The reader should allow time for absorption, reading aloud where possible, moving the eye and attention from drawing to text, allowing the mind and heart to make connections between them and the reader's experience. Glancing from text to drawing and back again allows the two to glance off of each other for an intensified impact.

There are stories implied in the poems and pictures, but neither means to tell a linear tale. They intend, rather, to recapture the mystics' experiences, to distill their lives. They want to be a faceted crystal, so that each reader who brings his or her own life to the images may find something recognizable and something new.

Mystics, poets, and artists learn to wait, to trust, and to rely upon the darkness, just as nature has always depended on it. Nature folds the dark into waiting periods for events like birth and dawn and harvest and sunset. It enables both mystical experience and the comprehension of it. Consequently, mystics often use nature imagery. In their texts, God is water, fire, darkness, light, birth, death, wind, stillness. Such universal images, rooted in nature, are likely to endure because they can speak to all peoples across the ages.

Thomas Merton said that more mystics are women because women are better at waiting. Judging from the imagery of the mystics, we think that women—for whatever reason—may merely be closer to nature than men are. Thus, they are more likely to have the language to express mystical experience.

The women encountered here have spoken to us in a special way. We hope that they speak to the reader as well.

From Darkness

to Light

Mary of Magdala

Magdala was two-and-a-half miles out of beautiful Tiberias on the Sea of Galilee. It was no backwoods hamlet but a town rich with wheat, the fishing harvest, pottery making, boat building, and a dye works. Despite the abundance around them, however, Magdala's people, like others in the Roman Empire, were subject to grinding poverty as they lost their land bit by bit to Roman taxation.

Mary of Magdala was the leading woman disciple in Jesus' company, a woman from whom "he had formerly cast out seven devils" (Mark 16:19). These devils banished by Jesus are usually connected with violent illness, like epilepsy, although we might also imagine their connection to the dark frustration felt by an imaginative young woman looking for some purpose beyond her society's expectation that she marry young and have many children. In other words, Mary may have been responding to yearnings similar to those of Jesus' male disciples.

Mary of Magdala accompanied Jesus' mother at the foot of his cross in the darkness and returned early on Sunday morning to see the brightness of the risen Lord. She then ran to give an account to the apostles who quickly labeled it an "idle tale." She, whom he had called and made into a faithful disciple, was the first witness to his Resurrection. Sometimes confused with the prostitute who wiped Jesus' feet with her hair and sometimes with the sister of Martha of Bethany, Mary of Magdala is better understood as one of the brave women who—like other disciples—left behind their homes and families and convention in order to follow the Master. Luke says that the women disciples provided for the followers of Jesus "out of their own resources" (8:30). We can imagine a group of capable women cooking food and providing shelter with their own funds or organizing a series of "covered-dish suppers" wherever they went. We can understand that their reward would be living in the presence of the Lord—"Rabboni" as Mary called him—who fed their need for meaning and a sense of freedom and light.

Mary of Magdala

Mornings,
    to escape the dye works' smoke,
I went to watch the fishers
throw out nets in hope,
haul them in, sometimes empty
as their children's bellies,
more often swelling with fish
that writhed against their fate.

    To fish and be free
    not like fish in the sea

I wanted to fling nets too,
spin them out like sparkling webs,
though I felt myself the fish
flailing about in search of
a rent in the net of my life
full of bowls and brooms.
My suitors said I was crazy
(the rabbis, "possessed"),
but my father merely shook his head
and let me scare them off.

  To fish and be free
  not like fish in the sea

The sea invited me beyond
the woman's precinct of the synagogue,
beyond the seasons' cycle,
a new child with each new year,
half of them dead before the next.
I could imagine myself on the ships,
triremes from Tyre and Babylon; longboats
meeting caravans at Tiberias.

 To fish and be free
 not like fish in the sea

His the most exotic cargo,
he saw my inner rooms,
gloomier than the caves of Galilee.
His first word banished my "possession."

My appetite more keen
than a child's for fish, I hungered
for the justice he drew with his words,
the freedom he was. He named me
fisher

> to fish and be free
> not like fish in the sea

They were few but stirring years.
At night, he wandered off to pray
and returned to serve the breakfast
we women cooked on an open fire. More
than once we fed multitudes. Then
we'd walk all day to the next town
or gather the other hungry at the synagogue
or in a field. I at his feet, his words
moved in my heart like a child in the womb.

> To fish and be free
> not like fish in the sea

On the way to Jerusalem,
I felt the net again,
not in my hands but closing in
on my struggle to swim in choppy sea.
You know how it turned out:
four of us standing there on Golgotha
with empty hands, only his mother's arms

holding my demons at bay.
The stone at Joseph's tomb, those two
in white shirts telling us not to fear
(What could they know of fear?)
and the gardener speaking my name
as he always did, part question,
part caress.

> To fish and be free
> not like fish in the sea

The men in their fear, poor fish,
reverted to treating us like women,
swore we told idle tales, even doubted
his cures of us. But they came around,
crept out of their garrets and cisterns.
I thought to return to Magdala,
to the beach and the roads he walked,
but his mother stayed in the city,
so now I fish here too
for the poor and the panicked
caught as I was
before he hauled me in

> to fish and be free
> not like fish in the sea

Clare of Assisi

(ca. 1198-1253)

Clare of Assisi, a lovely young noblewoman, grew up in a household of holy women living with knights who were addicted to feudal war games. Because of their wars, the child and her family became refugees at the age of six. Her early desire for voluntary poverty and chastity has been compared with that of the beguines, communities of medieval women who also created alternative social and economic structures so that they could live free for the service of God.

According to Clare's biographer, Ingrid Peterson, "Social status was the accepted form of identity in medieval society. As long as Clare was a noble woman she had an identity. But when she passed through the door of nobility, leaving her aristocratic state behind in order to join Francis and his brothers, Clare had no place in her society. Losing her class identity also meant releasing society's grip on her, with its restrictive roles and expectations of noble women. The doorway [through which Clare left her family] is symbolic of Clare's liminality which is essential for growth." Passing through the doorway led her from darkness to light.

Francis of Assisi came to Clare because he had heard about her holiness and complete commitment to God. (She had sold off her property, effectively taking herself out of the marriage market.) In 1212, while Francis was still trying to establish a brotherhood, Clare left her family home to begin a foundation of Poor Ladies at San Damiano, the church that Francis had built, possibly with financial assistance from Clare herself. She was joined at San Damiano by a number of noble women, relatives, and neighbors, also desiring to serve God as free women.

Clare and her community clung to poverty out of love for the poor Christ. She tended the sick at the risk of her own health. She also engaged in non-violent protest, refusing food when the pope forbade the brothers to preach at her monastery: she didn't want "corporal bread," she said, if she couldn't have "spiritual bread." When the Saracens invaded Assisi and actually penetrated their monastery enclosure, the sisters claimed that Clare, on her sick bed, prayed the enemy into fleeing "as if driven away." The Poor Clares, as Clare's community has come to be known, remain until today guardians of poverty and prayer.

The poem uses the sonnet form because the sonnet was born in Italy around the same time that Clare was living at San Damiano.

Chiara, thin and spinning, stirred no dust
in the Umbrian summer; in winter
wore no cloak but God's embrace, thought bitter
earthly food; lived in the liminal, just
like the light. She left home through the barred doors
and seized the altar cloth for sanctuary,
shearing her hair like her brothers'. Away
with suitors! No prayers for their courtly wars.

Her luminous guide, Lady Poverty,
led her to lepers, women, and the poor.
"The Lord reveals what is best to the least."
Now she abides, once again refugee,
eyes fixed on the light at the final door
that opens onto a hungerer's feast.

Kateri Tekakwitha

(1656-1680)

A Native American who retained her ancestral identity, Kateri Tekakwitha also became a Roman Catholic saint. Her mother, a Christian Algonquin abducted as a prisoner of war, married a Mohawk chief. Later, smallpox killed both of Kateri's parents and her brother and left a disfigured and partially blinded little girl to be reared by an uncle and aunts. Those caring for her were infuriated when their niece became a Catholic like her mother. In order to avoid marriage to a warrior, Kateri fled to a new Christian Iroquois village near Montreal when she was twenty years old. "I prefer the rapids to the net," she said, explaining her 200-mile trek on foot to Sault St. Louis. She bore an introductory letter from the French Jesuit who had baptized her; "I send you a treasure," he said, "guard it well."

Although Kateri could not see clearly at a distance, she retained vision enough to do exquisite craft work, beading designs into moccasins and leggings, plaiting corn leaves into shoes, and sewing shells and quills to quivers and skirts. Her name means "one who puts things in order." As a child, she would have undergone Iroquois puberty rites, carrying a little food and water into the wilderness and emerging as a full-fledged member of the Mohawks. Thus shaped by nature's solitude, she is rightly seen as a mystic of the wilderness and a patroness of ecology as well as peace.

Iroquois men (including the Mohawk) were warriors and town-builders who grouped their bark-covered houses in compounds inside palisades with corn and squash growing outside the walls. The older women chose the male leaders, grew the crops, and took seriously their control over reproduction. At least once, in protest, the women refused to engage in sexual intercourse with men who insisted on making war. The Iroquois also had some history of peace; in the fifteenth century a holy man preaching peace inspired the formation of the Five Nations Confederacy that brought together formerly warring Iroquois nations.

The Five Nations symbol was a huge tree beneath which all peoples could live in peace. Like the whole earth, the tree rode on the back of a turtle, and an eagle lived at the top of the tree to warn whenever peace was threatened. Kateri longed for this bright peace, and her choice of Christianity and virginity was an expression of her deep desire for her people's peace beyond the bloody darkness of war.

Kateri Tekakwitha's Dream Song

On the waving hills above the river
in the time of trillium and violets
the women plant the corn

I am "she who puts things in order"
tending the fire in the longhouse
mixing the sagamite
working the starry beads
into belts and moccasins

My people killed the Blackrobes
shook the deer hoofs and puffin beaks
rattled the quills
banged the drums
while blood ran from the palisades

On the waving hills above the river
in the time of trillium and violets
the women plant the corn

I went to the woods as a child
with small food and no salt
walked out to greet my loneliness
and returned a woman
who carved on the birch
the sign of the cross

Now I eat of the faithfulness of trees
Now I am a bark bowl
for God's flowing down
to wash the stained leggings
of him who wields the tomahawk

On the waving hills above the river
in the time of trillium and violets
the women plant the corn

My snowshoes never sink
on the whiteness of the field
when I go out to hear God in the wind
I sense the white man's wantonness
bearing his god of noise
leaving carcasses to rot

Though I see but dimly
as through a dark glass
like Jesus' friend who saw the moving trees

29

My fingers trace the veins on dappled leaves
　　our lives' patterns that the heart knows
　　　even when the eyes fade

On the waving hills above the river
　　in the time of trillium and violets
　　　the women plant the corn

Choosing the rapids over the net
　　like whitefish, the deer of the water,
　　　　I come to the Sault
　　　retrace the path of my mother
　　　　　Algonquin slave, my first baptizer
　　　　　　whose blue blanket Mary Mother wears

In the time of strawberries
　　we all caress the turtle's back
　　　the tree of peace grows from its shell
　　The eagle will circle
　　　when the lover of war comes again

I ride on the bright cloud of her nest

Water in

the Desert

Miriam, Sister of Moses

In the Book of Exodus (2, 15), Miriam is the older sister of Moses, watching over him in his basket among the reeds when Pharaoh's daughter finds him in the river. Cleverly, Miriam suggests the baby's own mother for a wet nurse. Years later, when the Israelites escape from Egypt, Miriam, now a prophetess, leads her people with her brothers Moses and Aaron, and after the parting of the Red Sea, she orchestrates a celebration of song and dance.

God often speaks to a people through prophets and prophetesses, but they frequently are vilified in the process. In the Book of Numbers (11, 12, 20), all three leaders question Moses' authority at some point. Moses wonders aloud why he is burdened with the care of a stiff-necked people. "Am I their mother?" he explodes in frustration. Seeing Moses' flaws, both Aaron and Miriam question his leadership, asking, "Is Moses the only one with whom the Lord has spoken? Has he not spoken with us as well?" They wish for a shared leadership as well as a shared vision.

After the Lord upbraids Aaron and Miriam for doubting Moses, who "alone is faithful," Miriam's skin turns "diseased and white as snow," a sign of leprosy. Despite Moses' pleas in her behalf, God banishes her from the camp for seven days, but the people do not strike camp until she returns. All three question, but only Miriam is punished. Some scholars see this as the authors' need to demote a woman who doubts patriarchal leadership. Or perhaps—since both ask the same question—Miriam is seen as more powerful and thus more threatening than Aaron.

Before coming into the Promised Land, all three leaders die, Miriam first, in the wilderness of Zin, a place without water. She dies before God tells Moses to strike a rock to get water for the complaining people, and the poem sees a connection between her death and the miracle of the water. Since Miriam's whole life has been associated with water (the Nile River, the Red Sea, the longing for it in the desert), her final gift to the people may have been the water that meant their survival.

EXODUS 2
We wove a basket, and I took my stand
nearby, ankle deep in water, the silver
fishes slivering around my feet
until she came, all white and indigo,
and saw the basket. My voice near
strangled by my cramping heart, I
stuttered that my mother was a wet nurse.
She nodded,
and a heron honked approval in the reeds.

EXODUS 15
We would have stayed from fear,
but the wind that blew the water up
blew us across the sea-bed, moist
and carpeted with reeds, other reeds
still swimming in the walls like eels.
Water had always been my friend.
After the crossing, women hiding
children's faces in their garments,
we never looked back
until the roaring and the soldier's screams.
Like me, the others had packed
tambourines in place of grain.
What is life without song?
I held mine high to dance:

"Sing to the Lord
covered with triumph!
Horse and rider
hurled into the sea."

NUMBERS 12

I had not thought there was a place so far
from water and the black earth where vines
and orange trees weave a shelter
against the overbearing light.
My brother saw God
but took too much on himself.
Aaron and I, could he have seen it,
spared him, heard out
the fear of wandering forever
that hardened their hearts.
Why did God punish me for saying it?
Never mind the white face. The terror
was God's own face turned from me, absent
like water on this trek into aridity,
this dark parade through blinding desert.
Exile from the camp pales beside
God's exile from me.
I long for that wellspring.

NUMBERS 20

To think of dying in the wilderness of Zin,
everyone around me wailing for water
as my soul has wailed for forty years.

They still don't know my final gift:
these stones will gush water.
My life is given for it,
their corn and figs and pomegranates
sprung from my loins,
juice of the generations.
And for me, at last, God's face.
I cross over to water too.

Julian of Norwich

(1342-1413)

Julian was an anchoress, one who lived and prayed alone in an anchorhold or small room attached to a church. The anchorhold had no door, except to an enclosed garden, though a window or squint allowed the anchoress to receive Holy Communion as well as gifts of food and petitions for prayers. An extant rule for anchoresses, *The Ancrene Riwle*, permitted walks in the garden as well as one cat per anchorhold to kill off mice.

Norwich was a seaport town that had, in Julian's day, a settlement of beguines, lay women establishing economically independent communities to free themselves for God and service. The presence of other independent church women might have encouraged Julian. The church of her anchorhold stood beside a busy road where the wagons of a new mercantile society—the England of Chaucer's *Canterbury Tales*—passed by constantly. People who had experienced death (in 1349, the bubonic plague swept the town), famine, the Hundred Years War, church schism, and the confusion stirred up by Wycliffe and the Lollards came to her anchorhold to pray with her and to be refreshed by the deep springs of her listening.

Julian herself experienced a series of visions that she records in her *Shewings*. There she speaks of God holding the world, no bigger than a hazelnut, that "lasts and always will because God loves it." She sees a Mother Christ giving birth to the world. Sin, she declares, is caused by ignorance and has no ultimate reality; it is, in fact, "behovely" or necessary because it brings self-knowledge to the sinner. Her view of the world runs counter to the bland optimism overlaying the new materialism and deep cynicism of her day.

The world she sees and describes is good because it is created and sustained by God. "All shall be well, and all manner of things shall be well," is her final word, a word that also speaks eloquently today, as T. S. Eliot understands when he alludes to it in the poem, "Little Gidding," part of his *Four Quartets*.

Julian of Norwich

They walled you up with last rites:
you wanted it, Anchoress,
the "deep drying" of God's pain.
"Today is my Doomsday." At night

outside on the old Norwich road
you heard the new wagons of greed,
the drunken sailor's curse, bells
on carts creaking to mass graves.

Others travelled to shrines—
Canterbury, Campostella—you
became one. In the anchorhold,
hearing Mass through a "squint,"
your name lost but a room gained,
a cat on your lap, you saw
that sin is "behovely"—the more
we sin, the more we're forgiven.

Like a good Buddhist, named it
ignorance: the servant who
stumbles in his haste to serve
merits a greater reward.

His master, your mistress, our
Mother Christ, body broken
birthing the hazelnut world
lasting because God loves it.

Like the Mother "forth spredyng"
love in creation, you knew
to seek is always to find. God
is closer than our own souls.

41

Thérèse of Lisieux

(1873-1897)

Thérèse Martin was born at Alençon, Normandy, to pious parents, a jeweler and a lacemaker. She was a cherished child, not much aware of the world beyond her family and their religious practices. Her mother died when she was four years old, and her three older sisters all mothered her intensely. When her sisters entered the cloistered Carmelite convent, Thérèse too decided to enter although she was only fifteen. Her father accompanied her to Rome in order to request a dispensation from the pope.

As a young girl, Thérèse prayed for an unrepentant murderer who, just before he was executed, kissed the wounds of Christ on the crucifix. She felt his contrition was an answer to her prayer. After she entered Carmel, she became the "spiritual sister" of a missionary, for whom she prayed and with whom she corresponded. When she was dying at the age of twenty-four, she said that she was glad to die before the age that young men were ordained to the priesthood, since she herself wanted to be a priest and would be refused ordination. Despite—or because of—her intense inner life, her horizon encompassed the needs of the wider church and people with lives quite unlike hers.

Although tall and healthy-looking, Thérèse died of tuberculosis. The convent was cold and damp; its regimen included fasting and other austerities. Thérèse never asked for special considerations. For the last months of her life, despite her great pain, she was not given morphine. Nevertheless, she finished dictating her autobiography, begun earlier at the behest of her superior, who was her own sister Pauline. A year after her death, Thérèse's *The Story of a Soul* was published and drew immediate interest from many.

In 1925, the pope canonized Thérèse of Lisieux as the Saint of the Little Way, and she became popularly known as the Little Flower. Even before her death, some of the sisters at Carmel had recognized her extraordinary ability to love in the midst of the tensions and minutiae of daily life. Love and littleness are her life's theme; as she put it, both the thimble and the glass can be full. Her own fullness of love she poured out in the bourgeois and pious desert where she lived her life.

The villanelle, a poetic form that wrings simplicity from artifice with a strict rhyming pattern and lines repeated at set intervals, suits the restricted but intense world in which Thérèse lived.

Was I waking up to the godhead in me
when my mother said I sang in her womb?
The torrent pulls all in its path to the sea.

Mothered by five in leaf-laced Normandy,
I learned from their love to make everywhere home
and greet everyone through the godhead in me.

With no compass besides eternity,
I fly to the heart of the world, not a tomb.
The torrent pulls all in its path to the sea.

In the deepest enclosure I shall be free
for even in darkness some flowers bloom
each springtime that wakes the godhead in me.

Jesus sleeps in my boat; hush, let him be.
Given over to him, I have become
the torrent that pulls in its path to the sea.

Children please parents most dearly in sleep,
filling both thimble and cup with love's sum.
Forever I wake to the godhead in me.
The torrent pulls all in its path to the sea.

Journey's Song

Teresa of Avila

(1515-1582)

Teresa de Ahumada was born at Avila, an ancient Castilian city with both Moorish and Jewish influences. One of nine children, she was only twelve years old when her mother died in childbirth. A favorite of her father, Teresa found herself placed by him in a convent school for safe-keeping. Known for her passionate and mischievous nature, she responded by entering another convent, against his wishes, when she was twenty. Around the same time, some of her brothers were setting off for adventure in the New World.

At the second, Carmelite convent in Avila, Teresa entertained frequent visitors and, like many of the nuns, treated her monastic environment like a salon. She never abandoned spiritual reading, however, and *The Confessions of St. Augustine* launched a new beginning in her spiritual life when she was nearly forty.

Her new way of prayer was quiet, visionary enough for her confessors to wonder how such a flawed person could be so gifted, passive enough to make the Spanish Inquisitors worry that she was heretically quietist when they read her *The Book of Her Life*. Her prayer led her to found a new monastery with fewer nuns (11 instead of 180), each with a room of her own, who would apply themselves seriously to mental prayer and the contemplative life.

Once the first foundation was accomplished, Teresa realized that others like it—independent of endowments from rich patrons—were an appropriate response to the religious conflicts raging in Northern Europe. So she began tireless journeys, usually riding in donkey carts, to found a number of new Carmels throughout Spain. This quest—often aided by her companion in mysticism and reform, John of the Cross— led her to involvement in royal politics, conflicts between church and state, threats of war between Spain and Portugal, and quarrels and litigations in her own family.

Teresa's greatest gift may be her writing, which describes in vivid imagery and astute psychological detail the approach of the soul to God, and God to the soul. She once heard the words, "Don't try to hold Me within yourself, but try to hold yourself within Me." In response, she articulated the modern understanding that mental prayer must underlie vocal prayer, that God gives the gifts, which cannot be evoked through clever techniques but may be prepared for through detachment, love of neighbor, and humility.

Considered one of the great women of history, Teresa of Avila has impressed her vibrant personality on the world and was the first woman named a Doctor of the Church. Her works include her *Life*, *The Way of Perfection*, and *The Interior Castle*. She says that she writes for people like herself—people like us—who have "souls and minds so scattered they are like wild horses."

Her brother:

>   Your dowry a will I scrawled
>   as I dashed off to plunder the New World,
>   you ransacked rooms richer than the Incas',
>   more inward,
>   unearthed by one more wayward
>   than conquistadores.

Her father:

>   For girlish indiscretions,
>   we tucked you in a convent school
>   you then chose from fear
>   of childbirth: your mother
>   died of her ninth.
>   That convent, a poor salon
>   infested with guests
>   you loved to love you,
>   boasted of its dark-eyed beauty,
>   curls slipping from her veil.

She:

>   A voice delivered me,
>   "No longer speak with men but angels."
>   I could answer only with silence,
>   then—
>   jostling along in donkey carts with venal guides,
>   laying over at filthy inns

("Life is a night spent in one"),
I stole into hovels
to convert them to convents
that freed women from peonage to the rich,
service to the dead.

Each had a room of her own.

The Inquisitors:
She teaches while denying it,
admits she writes
for minds "like wild horses."
We suspect women and converted Jews;
she may be both.

She:
In times of doubt the voice returns:
"You think about me.
Let me
worry about you."

The sisters:
Tambourine in hand, she sings
a song of fleas in woolen habits.
In ecstasy while frying eggs,
she regrets the spoiled meal.
From her we learned
the perfect metaphor for prayer:

God seeds, we water.
Beginners draw from wells

but arms grow tired;
later they can turn
the waterwheels on aquaducts
and then draw near
the spring itself
where the Lord Gardener
guides the flow.
Finally falls
the "heavenly water,"
tears,
on soil tilled by trial.

"One water draws down the others."

She:

No more warriors of God
fighting off distractions;
when hunger is satisfied,
attachments fall away.
"In the dark . . .
you just know he's there."

He:

Mi conquistadora, who are you?

She:

"Teresa of Jesus. And who are you?"

He:

"Jesus—of Teresa."

Emily Dickinson

(1830-1886)

Emily Dickinson, born to a prominent Amherst, Massachusetts family, lived her entire life in her father's house, except for a few years at school at Mount Holyoke College. Surrounded by family joy as well as family tension, her garden, her beloved dog Carlo, and the comings and goings of friends and famous visitors, she helped to manage a busy household and read deeply in science, religion, and literature. At an early age, she embraced solitude in order to preserve her intensity, "the brimfull feeling," for poetry and for questioning.

Growing up at the time of the evangelical revivals of America's Great Awakening, Dickinson felt herself alienated from her young friends who answered the "call" that she could not. For her, belief was a struggle, which she engaged in with steadfastness and ironic humor. She knew the stern God of the Calvinist Bible well (comparing this God to wild bears) and sought a more loving God. At the same time, she also knew Jesus as a fellow sufferer and experienced his words as "great bars of sunlight in many a shady heart."

Dickinson suffered many disappointments, the lack of an audience for her cryptic poetry perhaps the greatest of them, but she also knew that "the mere sense of living in joy is enough." As a woman, "the Wayward nun beneath the hill," she sacrificed for poetry and for the truth, redefining poetry in the process and simultaneously re-drawing "the Landscape of the Spirit." She claimed that her business was to love, and the invitation to love lights up her letters to family and friends.

Like most great poets, Emily Dickinson provides us with more questions than answers. As she puts it, "We both believe, and disbelieve a hundred times an hour, which keeps Believing nimble." Her "unfurnished eye" sees that the "Supernatural" is only the "Natural, disclosed." Her poetry is the record of an ecstatic inner journey; her employment of the word, sacramental. As her biographer Richard Sewall writes, "Although she never formally became a Christian, it was the promise of the Gospels and the vision of the Prophets that both strengthened her and, in long moments of doubt, haunted her throughout her life. This was the theme, 'stubborn as Sublime,' that she grappled with in poem after poem. She lived, it seems, in a state of wonder and hope."

Emily Dickinson

Sailor of "Circumference"
moored at home not sea—
far from any lighthouse
for Faith or Poetry

Your helm an upstairs window
for spying on the birds—
you heard the pious singing
songs that claimed you erred

Your Great Awakening
with "unfurnished eye"
saw Fluster and Betrayal
sinking ecstasy

So you sailed on with Carlo
and battened down—
keeping home and garden
to avoid the Town—

but crashed upon death
in wreck after wreck—
calling out "Love"
from a pitching deck

Tacking between the sun
and your forefathers
to keep "Believing nimble"—
not religion "like bears"

you lived for the words
that shadowed the Word—
sighting it slant—
that one "gold thread"

Maura "Soshin" O'Halloran

(1955-1982)

Born of an American mother and an Irish father and educated at convent schools and Trinity College, Dublin, Maura O'Halloran crossed borders of many kinds. By the age of twenty-seven, she had become a Zen master and acknowledged Bodhisattva, or Buddhist saint. As an adolescent, she practiced meditation and detachment from material things. Her passion for justice led her to volunteer social work in Ireland and Peru and to union organizing. At college, she distinguished herself in mathematics and linguistics.

While travelling in Japan, O'Halloran entered a Zen Buddhist monastery and, guided by a distinguished teacher, achieved enlightenment in six months. She continued her training for another two-and-a-half years, sitting in meditation for long periods of time, begging for the monastery, and working in the kitchen. Intending to return to Ireland

and begin a Zen center, she set out through Asia and died in a bus accident in Thailand. At her death, her teacher called her "the modern Dogen," after the great Buddhist master. Approximately a year before her death, she wrote:

> I'd be embarrassed to tell anyone, it sounds so wishy-washy, but now I have maybe 50 or 60 years (who knows?) of time, of a life, open, blank, ready to offer. I want to live it for other people. What else is there to do with it? Not that I expect to change the world or even a blade of grass, but it's as if to give myself is all I can do, as the flowers have no choice but to blossom. At the moment the best I can see to do is to give to people this freedom, this bliss, and how better than through zazen? So I must go deeper and deeper and work hard, no longer for me but for everyone I can help. . . . Thus I should also work politically, work to make people's surroundings that much more tolerable, work for a society that fosters more spiritual, more human, values. A society for people, not profits. What better way to instill the Bodhisattvic spirit in people?

O'Halloran's mother, Ruth, has gathered her daughter's letters and journals into a book, *Pure Heart, Enlightened Mind*. She believes that her daughter remained thoroughly Christian while embracing Buddhism. Others have called Maura O'Halloran the first Buddhist-Christian saint.

Haiku 5 alludes to her visit to a rural Japanese couple. The wife made a tea in "a long ritual of wiping and whirling the universe into a bowl" and serving it from "a huge tree trunk turned into a table" in their dirt-floored house. Haiku 6 refers to her Zen master's comment that in thirty years of students, O'Halloran was the only one to train as if to "abandon her life." The quotation in Haiku 8 is from her teacher after her death.

1
Round eyes from the West
put on the Buddha nature
Emptiness is all

2
Late in the kitchen
deep sighs from the weary self
Empathy for all

3
The bird in the tree
shakes wetness from its feathers
sings to the quiet

4
Four nights of zazen
The first, all things are Buddha
The last, all things are

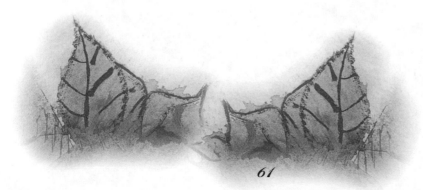

5

Dark room of damp earth
A woman pours out the world
on tree trunk table

6

Not striving, she lives
abandons her life with "no
choice but to blossom"

7

For one thousand days
Dogen sat on the mountain
Maura sleeps there now

8

She saves the masses
Can I "possibly express
my astonishment?"

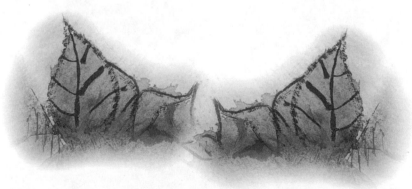

Consumed

by Fire

Mechtild of Magdeburg

(ca.1207-1294)

A great medieval German writer and one of the first to write in the vernacular, Mechtild of Magdeburg was well born and well educated. "Half poet, half seer" according to Evelyn Underhill, Mechtild was probably influenced by the romantic poets or *minnesingers* of her time more than by religious writers. Dante read her work, which is reflected in his "Paradiso." Some scholars think that she is the Matilda of his Earthly Paradise.

Although theologically sound, Mechtild ran afoul of the clergy because she criticized both them and the church and because she was associated with the beguines, lay women who sought to remain independent of clerical control and provide economic and spiritual support for poorer women. A feminist before the era of feminism, she wrote to a correspondent, "You are surprised at the masculine way in which this book is written? I wonder why that surprises you?"

At the age of twelve, she received her first "greeting from God" and begged to be reviled as Jesus was. She got her wish and became, as she called herself, "a post or target at which people throw stones." In her old age, blind and sick, she was taken in by the Benedictine sisters at the abbey at Helfta, whom she encouraged to write about their experience of God.

Mechtild's own image of God, captured in her great work *The Flowing Light of the Godhead*, was God as a flame or river of fire filling the universe. The *minne-flut* or divine "flood of love" that overcomes every soul reflected her own joyous spirit. Until she died, she proclaimed the fluidity of God in images of water, milk, wine, tears, blood, honey, and molten gold. She saw the connectedness of all things in a God whose compassion overcomes power.

No heights.
God greeted you at twelve,
you begged to be reviled
and joined Beguines
escaping marriage bonds
and priests,
the church a girl
with filthy skin.

A minne-flut of liquids,
god, and fire,
"like needles to a magnet
you shall come."
The magnet pulled you down
into the valley
but grace flows
to low places.
"Lie down in the Fire,
See and taste the Flowing."

A post they stoned,
you sank and cooled,
blind at Helfta in the end,
living with saints
but never getting the name.
"If thou has the weights,
I have the gold."
It does not perish in this Fire.

Catherine of Genoa

(1447-1510)

Caterina Fieschi Adorna came from a proud Guelph family in the proud city of Genoa. She embraced prayer and penance as a child but was married off at fifteen to a profligate and blatantly unfaithful husband. For the first five years of her marriage, she suffered severe depression. For the next five, she tried to lose herself in her role as a socialite.

At the age of twenty-five, Catherine prayed for illness in order to escape her life. Moving into confinement and silence, she returned to God and learned to live with a double awareness of bliss and suffering in the image of the crucified Christ. Subsequently, she went out into the streets to care for the poor and the sick and eventually was asked to administer the Pammetone, a private hospital for the poor of Genoa.

Eventually, Catherine's husband went into bankruptcy and had a conversion that led him to join in her work. They lived as brother and sister, moving into two rooms at the hospital, where Catherine also cared for his child and his sick mistress. When the plague ravished Genoa, Catherine personally nursed many of its victims and, as an administrator, extended the hospital's capacity by setting up around it tents made from sails.

A solitary surrounded by people with immense needs, Catherine epitomizes the ecstatic who never desists from outer work. As she grew older and found companions in her work and in her spiritual search, she seemed less driven by inner conflicts and began to speak and write of her experiences of God. In *The Spiritual Dialogue*, she records that God is Pure Love the soul can put on by allowing grace to enter and defeat its own Self Love. She views the spiritual life as a process or pilgrimage towards Pure Love where the pilgrim's vehicle is perfect trust in God.

Catherine's teaching has had a profound influence on both Roman Catholic and Protestant teaching about spirituality. John of the Cross, Francis de Sales, Vincent de Paul, John Henry Newman, Baron von Hugel, Isaac Hecker, the founders at Brook Farm, Phoebe Palmer, and others looked to Catherine for example. Lay people, in particular, have seen in her a model.

One contemporary observed that when a friar told her that he was wedded to religion and she to the world, Catherine became so agitated that her hair burst from its headdress as she responded emphatically, "That I cannot love God as much as yourself, you can never make me believe." As she had once been eaten up by depression and anxiety, she was ultimately consumed by the fire of Pure Love and felt confident of her place in Love.

Why not a wooden pillow?
    asks the child.
You marry me to mend a feud,
    cries the girl.
I flee to parties and depression.

Embrace God,
    asserts the woman.
Why not become fire?
    Become a saint
to keep sane. Enter confinement:
    birth yourself.

When he "tugged with a glance,"
I ceased the great refusal,
began to grow.

More covered with sin
    than "a cat with hairs,"
yet I faulted that friar who faulted
    my not being a nun:
"Even as a camp follower I'd love you."

In mid life, Purgatory.
    Does fire refine?
Scrub the houses of the poor,
    wash their vermin-ridden rags,
knead, then eat, the bread of pain,
    bold betrayal by a husband.

I counted the hospital's florins,
    kept its books
kept a closet there
    for prayer.
Become the prayer.

"Call Jesus," I told the woman with plague
    whom I kissed.
The sick came on like waves,
    so I gazed at the harbor
and ordered up the shipyard's sails
    for tents.
        Did the white sail of your soul
        unfurl itself at the head of the fleet
        that skirmished with death
        in its perilous passage?
Today
you take our breath away.
    When bombs blew
    the hospital to bits in World War II,
    they merely compounded your fire.

Edith Stein

(1891-1941)

Edith Stein had a happy childhood in a large family living near the lumberyard in Breslau that her mother managed after Edith's father died. The family recognized Edith's intellectual gifts and supported her education and scholarly work. Secular and Jewish, they were also patriotic Germans who supported the Fatherland in World War I. Edith interrupted her studies to work in a military hospital or *lazaretto* at Mährisch-Weisskirchen. She nonetheless completed her

Doctorate in Philosophy in 1918 at the University of Freiburg where she was assistant to the phenomenologist Edmund Husserl, whom she called "the Master." She wrote her doctoral dissertation on the nature of empathy.

After the war, Edith failed to get a university appointment. Her gender, her Jewishness, and the novelty of her philosophical approach all seem to have worked against it. In 1922, despite the pain it caused her family, Stein was baptized a Roman Catholic. For the next ten years, she taught at a Dominican Sisters teachers' college in Speyer and acquired an international reputation as a lecturer in pedagogy. In 1933, she was named a Docent at the German Institute for Scientific Pedagogy in Munster.

At the time of the *Umsturz*, the Third Reich's coming to power with its overt restrictions against Jews, Edith's publisher reneged on an agreement to bring out her book. Feeling thereby freed from scholarly responsibilities, Edith decided to enter the cloistered Carmelite monastery at Cologne. There she received the religious habit on April 15, 1934 at the age of forty-three and took the name Sister Teresa Benedicta of the Cross. There she also continued her work in philosophy while watching the Nazi encroachment. Her brothers and sisters began emigrating from Germany, and she joined in prayer the priests and religious being imprisoned.

At the end of 1938, Edith fled to the Carmelite convent at Echt, Holland, and was followed there by her sister Rosa Stein, who had also become a Catholic. At Echt, Sister Teresa Benedicta formally offered herself as a propiation for peace. In 1940, the Nazis invaded Holland, and she began hearing of the detainment of friends and family members in Germany. When she had to register with the Dutch authorities, the Carmelites began arrangements for her transfer to a convent in Switzerland. By December 1941, however, the Occupation Forces had declared all non-Aryan residents in the Netherlands stateless and was threatening to deport them.

On July 20, 1942, Stein's local bishop, along with four other bishops, signed a pastoral letter of protest against the deportation of Jews that so enraged the Nazis that they arrested Catholic Jews, among them Edith Stein, on August 2. Within a week, the prisoners were deported and killed in Auschwitz.

Edith Stein was a brilliant student and philosopher, a frank and encouraging friend, and a teacher with a special gift for drawing out the promise of her students. She felt that the younger generation had "passed through so many crises—it can no longer understand us, but we must make the effort to understand them." She had a joyful family life and—despite hardship incurred in finding her way around prejudice—a satisfying career. She embraced the Carmelite life in order "to live in the inner sanctum of the church and to represent those who must labor outside." Her model in that was Esther, taken from her people in order to stand up for them.

Until the end, Sister Teresa Benedicta remained calm and cheerful, solicitous of others who needed consolation. From the camp at Westerbork, Holland, just before she left for Germany, she wrote to the sisters at Echt: "Now we have a chance to experience a little how to live purely from within." Destroyed by the most systematically murderous forces of our century, she remained undefeated in bringing her spiritual energy to bear on the evil.

The train that transported Sister Teresa Benedicta, her sister Rosa, and other Jews from Holland stopped at numerous German cities and towns on the way to Auschwitz. The poem follows the route of the train, recalling Edith's life at the various places and imagining what she might have remembered as she passed through. At Schifferstadt and Breslau, observers sighted her on the train.

1. Echt:

We came here at night,
crossing the border before
word of the death of friends,
our brother and sister at Theresienstadt
(Mother, thank God, died last year),
and they destroyed my letters at Cologne
before the convent went up in flames.

> *I leave with pounding in my brain*
> *like the pounding at the door,*
> *one male voice raking across*
> *the convent quiet, seeking the stateless,*
> *me, who did not flee to Switzerland*
> *because the paperwork was slow.*
> *So now we take the final journey*
> *of those who weep in silence,*
> *hoping against the evidence*
> *that the family will find a home.*

2. Freiburg:

> *The train does not stop here,*
> *peels through time's darkening skin,*
> *taunting the endless student days,*
> *philosophy in green and brown rooms,*
> *rambles in the Hartz mountains.*

Here I met "the Master" Husserl
who later let me see
that all who seek the truth
seek God. Enchantingly malicious
someone called me then,
too idealistic to be kind.
But I learned to "give in,
in all that is not unjust"
and wrote about the gift of loving
persons more than what they do.

Here "student life was blown to bits"
by a war so ruinous it had to be short
(in fact, was merely prelude)
but I formed a habit for crisis:
go on with your life,
prepared to halt at any moment,
as Hector commended his wife to housework
when he said his last farewell.

Like shapes from clouds
the work came clear.

3. Schifferstadt:

A "lady in dark clothes" calls
out from the transport
to tell her friends
that she has gone to Poland.

4. Speyer:

Through the rows of lights

from low houses, into the station
lumber the dark cars heaving
with the muted sobs of children.

Here I taught girl children
to claim their "swan-destiny,"
as I learned the script for sacrifice,
"the urgency of my own *holocaustum*."

The word provokes a chill.

Here I chose the Church
of sinners, lost my friends.
    My mother wept. Yet
"life begins anew each morning."
Reaching out to Husserl from new ground,
translating Newman "like a window,"
I was freed to be a Carmelite
standing in for sinners
when the *Umsturz* blocked the obvious
and the publisher lost courage.

5. Breslau:

> *A soldier from Cologne, a new*
> *recruit to form a postal unit*
> *in the eastern zone, waits*
> *in the depot as the door slides*
> *open on a freight car*
> *packed with people cowering.*
> *The stench is overpowering.*

> *A woman in nun's clothing*
> *says to him, "This is my beloved*
> *hometown. I will never see it*
> *again. We are riding to our death."*

In the first war we blundered through
though private life was gone.
Mother said we'd beat the Russians back
with broomsticks. She did it all
when Father died. We could always return
to the spacious rooms near the lumberyard.

No one can imagine our security
before. After, only shifting circumstance.
I wrote, to prove a Jew hath eyes,
of my large and fractious family,
my dear mother, I your youngest,
your beloved. How Hans and I would dance!
I whistled when I solved math problems. Latin
seemed my mother tongue. I longed
to serve the Fatherland
but could not gloat at French defeat.

6. Mährisch-Weisskirchen:

> *The box car wheels,*
> *raw nerves along the tracks,*
> *screech beneath the station sign*
> *we read in light that*
> *slices through the cracks.*

Poles and Germans,
Magyars, Czechs, Bavarians:
all were the same at the *lazaretto*,
all dying men
or those who'd live because of food and cigarettes,
help with writing letters home.
I postponed my Greek exam
and took two books,
Homer and Husserl's *Ideen*,
fighting the lice in the linens,
and winning the day for cleanliness.

7. Auschwitz:

   "So far I have been able to pray gloriously."

Accepting the invitation I could
not refuse, I arrive where I never
was before, though I had heard of
the "great grace" of prisoners
who accept in the name of all,
Esther before the king,
and the Crucified "at every front,
in every place of sorrow."

Born on the Day of Atonement,
the child called by her sisters
"a book sealed with seven seals,"
dies on a black fast day,
the *scientia crucis* achieved.

Heil im Unheil:
where sin is, grace abounds.

Speaking Truth

to Power

Catherine of Siena

(1347-1380)

Catherine Benincasa, the twenty-fourth of twenty-five children in a mercantile family of Siena, was a bit of a show-off. She took a vow of virginity at the age of seven, and to thwart suitors, scalded herself and cut off her hair at the age of fifteen. She affiliated with the Mantellate, a group of women—mostly local widows—who served the needy and lived at home under the direction of Dominican friars.

For three years after she donned the Dominican habit, Catherine remained in her room praying and somehow learning to read. At twenty-one, she began her years of nursing and social service and teaching others from her experience of God. Her abstinence from food and sleep accelerated as political tensions increased in church and state and her own involvement in them grew. Some have called her a "social mystic"; her biographer Suzanne Noffke names her, rather, a "mystic activist." Whatever label is given her, she remains a model for integrating prayer and the active life.

Catherine's love for truth, experienced directly in her visions, led her to defend the papacy in its feuds with the Italian city-states. With some naivete, she helped to preach a crusade, attempted to reform the clergy, and begged the pope to return from Avignon to Rome. In the last she was successful, but on a few occasions political factions took advantage of her good will. A dedicated group of men and women called Caterinati followed *la dolcissima mamma della bella brigata*, "the gentlest mother of the beautiful brigade."

In *Enduring Grace*, Carol Lee Flinders speaks of the fairy-tale quality of some mystics' lives. Catherine can readily be seen as a Cinderella fleeing from her family to live forever after with her prince charming, Jesus; this is how the poem views her. Exuberant in her relationships with God and other people, Catherine makes a grand heroine. Her visits with her lover on the roof, their exchange of hearts, his gift of a red garment from the wound in his side, her laughter after struggles with devils like "the Old Pickpocket," her courage in confronting ecclesiastics, her fasting from food and sleep: all are the stuff of high drama.

Having learned to read at age twenty, to write at thirty, Catherine wrote *The Dialogue*, one of the great and most readable books describing the experience of God. She then died at thirty-three. Besides being a saint, she is that rare woman proclaimed a Doctor of the Church.

What happy ending to this fairy tale?

The family made her its maid
when she scalded herself at the spa
the better to contemplate la Verita.
Then, Cinderella at the spit,
she rolled in embers, ecstasy,
until her father saw the white dove
above her head
and gave her back her room
with permission to give alms
from the family stores.
Her brothers locked their doors.

For three years
dunned by demons,
she learned to laugh
at the puffed-up dragons:
"Don't be afraid of the Old Pickpocket."

Intense as red Siena wine,
she wore an iron waist chain
and learned to read. Christ
pulled from his heart's wound
no glass slipper but
a red cloak, warm,
invisible to most
(Those who have eyes to see, let them).

They walked arm in arm on the roof,
praying the psalms,
and he placed his heart in her breast.
It beat louder than her own.

"You are she who is not," he said.
"I am He who is."

No carriages gave exit.
Later than many a midnight
she pleaded with wife-beating husbands
and parents with grudges enshrined in their wills,
challenged climbing churchmen,
condemned the daily wars of the Tuscan League.
No longer needing food or sleep,
she nursed those dying of plague,
leaning for their last words.

La dolcissima mamma della bella brigata
ordered the pope to return to Rome.
He did. Penitents poured from the hills.

At thirty she learned to write
in the vulgar tongue,
pronouns and tenses at odds,
parentheses within parentheses,
sentences left—like the meat on the spit—
undone,
by a prophet with coals at her tongue.

When *la beata popolana* died,
housework and healing squeezed from her being
"kneaded into Christ,"
they say that her soul left Rome
and stopped at a friend's in Siena
to prepare a meal
before she, happily ever after,
burst into God.

Sojourner Truth

(1797-1883)

The daughter of an African mother from whom she learned about an all-seeing God in Nature, Sojourner Truth was born Isabella the slave. She was six feet tall and a powerful personality who enchanted or confounded everyone who met her. She liberated herself from slavery in 1827 and thereafter worked to liberate other slaves and women as well as her own son, illegally sold to an Alabama family. Converted to Christianity in her twenties, she changed her name, wore simple Quaker dress, and became a mendicant preacher.

Early on, Isabella liked to pray outdoors, loudly, and to participate in Pinkster, an African feast much like Pentecost, celebrated on the plantations with song and dance. There she once had a vision of an all-powerful God who could annihilate her. Wishing for one who could speak to this overwhelming God for her, she heard a voice say, "It is Jesus." She had never heard of him. In pursuit of this friend, not a master like the all-knowing God who resembled her slave masters, the illiterate Sojourner asked children to read the Bible to her because she could request that they re-read as often as she wanted. She concluded that the Bible was truth, although mingled with opinions and suppositions!

Sojourner Truth spoke at many anti-slavery rallies in the 1840s. She desegregated Washington, D.C., street cars during the Civil War; that action cost her a permanently dislocated shoulder. She recruited "colored troops" for the Michigan regiment and helped ex-slaves to relocate, lobbying the federal government for land to be made available to them. She personally cared for old slaves that the New York Dutch expelled to the woods to die.

At the 1851 Women's Rights Convention, Sojourner Truth delivered her famous "Ain't I a Woman?" speech in her typically robust fashion. On another occasion, warned that if she spoke, the building would be burned down by protestors, she replied, "Then I will speak to the ashes." At times she quelled rowdy crowds with her singing, and she knew her audience: "The other preachers have the sheep, *I* have the goats. And I have a few sheep among my goats, but they are *very* ragged." She remains the outstanding African-American religious leader in the period after the Civil War.

"I will not allow
my life's light
to be determined by
the darkness around me."

"I'm going home
like a shooting star."

Your African mother
taught a God
who hears all and sees all
and lives with the stars
in the vault of heaven.

On an island
in a stream,
motherless
you wove an arch
from a nearby willow.
Beneath it
shaded from the vault
you prayed your life:
the dank cellar,
the household of eyes,
your own son sold South,
the old slaves left
in the woods to die.

At Pinkster
at a former master's
the Great One whispered
there was no place
where He was not.
You feared his "look"
and thought to be annihilated
as one "blows out a lamp."

> *"O God,*
> *I did not know*
> *you were so big."*

You too were big
so tall some called you man.
You bared your breasts
to show that you'd had milk,
had given it to children
mostly not your own.

> *"Ain't I a woman? . . .*
> *I have heard the bible*
> *and have heard that Eve*
> *caused man to sin. Well,*
> *if woman upset the world,*
> *do give her a chance*
> *to set it right. . . ."*

A light to prostitutes
and former slaves

who paid a homeless price
for victory,
you held back mobs
and dared conductors
to throw you off
their white street cars.

When Frederick Douglass said
the race would rise
by the power of its own right arm,
you asked, "Is God Almighty dead?"

With so many masters
making claims
how could a Master
claim your heart?

But Jesus had come
as mild and lovely friend
poised between you
and the "look."
Terror fled before him
and the world was willow-arched
again,
wick-trimmed and luminous,
with stars like gentle fires
lightening the firmament.

Simone Weil

(1909-1943)

Simone Weil and her brother André, as children called "the beauty" and "the genius," grew up in Paris with their loving and distinguished parents who were secular Jews. At the age of three, when given a ring, Simone commented, "I do not like luxury." Her path was set.

Here, the five sections of the poem refer to five photos reproduced in Simone Petrement's biography of Weil. Section I looks at the relationship between Weil and her brother, the games they played like "the door in tar," and the compassion they learned to practice by—among other things—sending their chocolate rations to soldiers in World War I. Later, Simone would experience war directly by joining the Republican cause in the Spanish Civil War, where she was severely burned while cooking and where she was appalled by the violence on all sides.

Section II describes Weil as a student of the famous philosopher Alain at the Lycée Henri IV. When she later matriculated first in her class at the *Ecole Normal Supérieure*, Simone de Beauvoir was second. Despite the severe migraine headaches afflicting her from the age of twelve, Weil disciplined herself through study and meditation. (Her definition of prayer is absolute attention to God.) In 1938, she visited the Benedictine Abbey at Solesmnes, famous for its Gregorian chant, and received a profound revelation of God's love. It came while she recited George Herbert's poem "Love," a text she turned to for the rest of her life.

Section III evokes Weil's teaching career. She taught philosophy in Lyons and in Auxerre, where her controversial methods led to the abolition of her position. Re-assigned in Rouanne and Bourges, she acquired a reputation for being an atheist and a communist, but her students were academically successful.

In Section IV, the allusions involve Weil's experiences as a laborer. She identified with workers and believed in physical labor as the spiritual core of a well-ordered life. In 1934, she took her first break from teaching to work at the Alsthom electrical factory in Paris. She also worked as a packer at Carnaud for one month (dismissed because she was too slow), at Renault for three months (she left exhausted), and at farms and vineyards in France and Italy.

Section V speaks of World War II and Weil's death. In 1942, she emigrated with her family to the United States. Attending daily Mass in New York and conceiving a plan to lead a nursing squad at the front, she prevailed upon a friend to help her get to England. There she worked for the French government in exile and continued to lobby for her return to France. At this time, she wrote *The Need for Roots*, a prophetic analysis of modern life. Partly because she refused food and medical rations in order to identify with victims of the war, she died of tuberculosis and starvation. She is buried in Ashford, Kent. Albert Camus called her "the only great spirit of our time."

Whatever else Weil was doing, she was always up late writing, keeping journals, sending off articles to leftist publications, arguing with friends in bistros. Among her brilliant works are *The Need for Roots*, the essay on "*The Iliad* As A Poem of Force," and two collections published posthumously, *Gravity and Grace* and *Waiting for God*.

I. With André at Mayenne

A child holds her brother's hand on a sunlit path:
beauty to his genius, someone said.
You declaimed Cyrano and chose the door
in tar over the door in gold, sending
your chocolate to adopted soldiers. Yours
came to visit once, soon was killed in action.
Later, in Spain, did you think of him
as you hunched in the mud under the plane's roar?

You recoiled from touch, but the taste for truth
ripened to hunger, would not
let you eat stones.

II. Henri IV Cagne

In Alain's class the rare woman, hatless
among the brushed suits and careful ties.
Nineteen and angular like your reasoning
and beloved geometry, inclined
to the "forthrightness of a boy"
your mother taught, you forbade yourself weakness
and decided to postpone love
until justice levelled the plain.

Other love bade you welcome at Solesmnes
though each note of the chant
beat at the migrainous flesh
you heaped in a pile
to attend to the sound.

III. With Students at Rouanne

One in snow and one in sun.

Your too small hands and wrists folding
into your sweater, beside the giant fir
bending under the snow, you stand
with your students nearly your age,
a dark figure in the white beauty,
and query the camera.

In the park, in spring or fall,
the black and white again,
light strained
through the leaves, and all
of you bent to books,
rapt by them, no one
noticing the camera or the light
like a bowl for your bodies.
The trees blaze,
flames to your candles below.

When did you become light?

IV. Renault Worker I.D. Card

Ticket to experiment with truth
Ticket to affliction that will kill your youth
A white blouse the first day, then blue,
    and apron stained with oil

The machine speeds up to cut your wages
"the problem of eating" will arise
Place the bobbins in the furnace pierced with holes
and let the furnace pierce your hands
and let the flames pass through
Fall asleep on the subway at night
Goad yourself on like a beast of burden in the
morning
Look for a job lost because you can't stop thinking
"painful to walk so much when one hasn't eaten"
Necessity mothers slavery not invention
By Sunday
only "shreds of ideas"

The worst: no camaraderie among the workers.
You sort the iron to smaller piles
so they can better carry them. But only once,
in the copper foundry, smiles.

V. A France Combattante Pass

Living in London against your will
and scheming to get to the war.
Aching to be potatoes
for those who starved,
you refused food
and died without the final pass
you might have had,
for a railway car to the East.

Thea Bowman

(1938-1990)

Granddaughter of a slave and the daughter of a Mississippi doctor, Thea Bowman grew up in an African-American family that lived among the poor. "During the first fifteen years of my life," she said, "I saw more of poverty, filth, disease, and suffering than many people see in a lifetime, and I learned that it is not a sacrifice to go without a few meals or bear a stench, fatigue, or a little dirt for someone you love." She thought of herself as a child of "old folks" still in touch with her elders, who taught her survival skills and wise sayings like "If you're scared, keep on steppin'." Her message to those who receive from others was, "Don't pay me back. Help somebody else."

At an early age, Bowman became a Roman Catholic and eventually a member of the Franciscan Sisters of Perpetual Adoration. She found convent life "cold and white" but felt that the God who had called her would also send her home if need be. Assigned to teach high school and college, the young nun earned her doctorate in English Literature at the Catholic University of America, writing her dissertation on St. Thomas More and spiritual comfort. There she also began to explore the oral tradition of early English literature and the American spirituals.

As a young person, Bowman was shy and eager to learn. As she grew in age and grace, she more boldly shared her gifts as a singer and dancer and spoke about the undervaluing of African Americans and women in church and society. "I like being black. I like being myself, and I thank God for making me my black self," was her theme. Once she "decided to come fully functioning" to her church and the world, she urged her black audiences to remember that they too were whole and could "stop being ashamed that our history included slavery. We didn't enslave ourselves. Somebody else enslaved us. Let the people who created slavery answer to God for it, and let us thank God for the cultural and faith traditions that enabled us to overcome it."

Bowman continued to work, to preach, and to sing after she was diagnosed with incurable cancer. Her dying, like her living, radiated joy. She addressed the assembled U. S. Roman Catholic bishops not long before she died, challenging them to give full range to the gifts of women and black people. A scholar and an inspiring teacher, she moved gracefully between the academy and the streets and did more to inspirit the African-American Roman Catholic community than any other twentieth century leader.

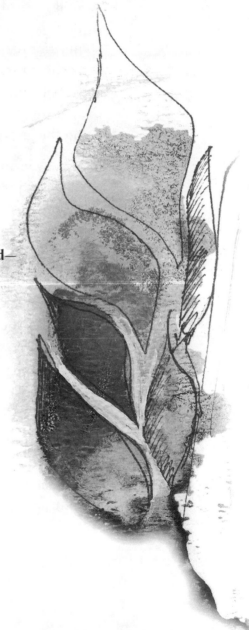

An "ole folks chile,"
all eyes and ears,
I heard music everywhere:
women hung the wash
singing Sunday hymns,
chain gangs worked the road
to the rise and fall
of response and call.

They crucified my Lord—
    crucified my Lord—
and he never said a mumbling word—
    never said a mumbling word.

That burden haunted me.
I carried its refrain
to the cool white convent
where we walked and slept
in certain, single file
and sometimes I felt
like a motherless child
light years from my home.

If anybody asks who you are—
    who you are—
tell them—
tell them, "I'm a child of God."

In the dry spaces
songs welled up,
flowers in my mouth,
milk for the motherless,
answers to pale prayer.
Now I dance to the thrum
that God beats out
on the justice drum.

If I a woman can't preach in the church—
**   can't preach in the church,**
I'll preach—
I'll preach in the neighborhood.

A granddaughter of slaves,
I'm kept unfree,
mere stepdaughter
in my own country,
a woman in shadows
the church can't see.
That justice may come
I shout jubilee.

Wake up in the morning—
Wake up—
and smile—
and smile at God.

The Open

Door

Rahab of Jericho

Rahab lived in Jericho when Joshua was trying to lead the Jewish people into the Promised Land. The Book of Joshua calls her a harlot or prostitute, but she may have been merely an innkeeper. (Visitors to either an inn or a house of prostitution would have failed to arouse public attention.) She offers the Jewish spies lodging, she apparently stands as mistress of her own house, and she can command her extended family to gather around her there.

When Joshua's scouts come to her house, Rahab recognizes in them a fearlessness lacking in her own people, the Canaanites, who live in terror of the approaching Israelites. "Your coming has left no spirit in any of us," she tells the spies. She senses that their Jewish god must be superior to the baals of her people, decides to believe in Yahweh, and then conceals the spies on the roof. If the Jews will promise to spare her family the coming bloodshed, she says, she will not betray them.

The spies give Rahab a scarlet cord to fasten at her window as protection for her family. When the Israelites attack the city, circling it for seven days until the walls fall, her family is spared and settles among the Jews. She herself becomes the mother of Boaz, who marries Ruth. Out of their line comes David, the ancestor of Jesus.

The Epistle to the Hebrews commends Rahab's faith; the Book of James, her works. The early Church saw in her a figure of itself, saving the family of faith, and in the scarlet cord, a figure of the blood of Christ. Others might find in her a symbol of all those risk-taking women who make possible through their belief and their courageous action the victories of heroes. Without her willingness to collaborate, could Joshua have won the battle of Jericho?

Joshua 2, 6; Hebrews 11:31; James 2:24-25

They came to the door at night,
putting themselves in my hand
like a wren in the palm;
fearless, unlike the miller
whose fingers trembled,
the salt vendor who looked to the hills
before he spoke.

I knew them for God's spies
and had not much to hide or lose
in a city that named me harlot
because I kept an inn
to keep my family.

When the loud knocks came at the door,
I lied to the city,
hid the spies under the flax
spread on the roof to dry,
praying it would not make a shroud.
They spoke softly
like doves in branches,
and I knew what truth sounds like.

When I said to them
the presence of God casts out fear,
they looked me up and down in disbelief,
then swore that my dear ones, gathered
into my nest, would be saved.
One took a scarlet cord from his waist,
red antidote to blood, and I tied it
in the window that they climbed out,
scuttling down a rope along the wall.

Later we learned the river gave way
like the reed sea. One morning
we woke to the ram's horns
piercing the fog of fear.
They dizzied us
circling the city.
Children ran along the wall
pointing to the ark and trumpets,

but their elders drank more fear:
locksmiths working overtime,
the vendor of salt barring his stores.

I brooded on the secret
that freedom begins outside the wall.
At last they came in a shout,
stunned the city to subjection
and spared only my own.
I would not have chosen so,
but they said their jealous God
would have no Canaanites but me.

Now I wear the red cord around my neck,
going about the city with respect.
My inn is open like the gates,
and I sing with the birds on the roof
while I wait for a son
who will also embrace a stranger.

Rose of Lima

(1586-1617)

Born into the large Olivas Verdes family as Isabel, Rose was re-named for her beauty by her Spanish father and her mother, a descendant of Incas. When her father lost his fortune, Rose became the family's sole support, selling her intricate needlework with its depictions of flowers, birds, and butterflies, usually on altar linens. Her parents hoped she would marry well, and so she learned to wear lovely clothes, write verses (like the one in the poem that puns on the family name), and play stringed instruments. She went on *paseo* (taking a walk to be seen) with her mother and brother but ultimately refused marriage, desiring instead a life of penance and service to the poor. Like Catherine of Siena, she became a Third Order (lay) Dominican. A working woman, she lived in the world.

113

Despite its image as a city of church bells and flowers, Lima was populated mostly by Indians and slaves, many of them women laboring in the households of the rich. Rose, an herbalist who also invoked the aid of Jesus the *mediquito*, opened a clinic for Indians, servants, and poor spinster relatives of the wealthy in a room that she rented in her parents' home. It was the first free clinic in the New World.

She also created a garden room where she could retreat for solitude. She had dreams and visions of Jesus and communicated with flowers and animals. Mosquitoes, she claimed, would not bother her at prayer because she had struck a deal whereby she would refrain from killing them. Legend has her protecting the city from threatened disaster, at the hands of either pirates or Dutch heretics! Her reputation for mysticism attracted the attention of the Inquisition. Although one of her spiritual advisors had said that Rose had "a gravity alien to women," the Dominican inquisitors concluded that she was not learned enough to be capable of dangerous error!

Considered the founder of social services in Peru, Rosa de Santa Maria Olivas Verdes had a gift for organization and a deep love of beauty. Socially cast as a dependent woman, she nevertheless made a room of her own—with space for God and the poor. Appropriately, she has been called the Flower of the New World and the Patroness of All the Americas.

Rose of Lima

On the altar
your embroidered birds
perch on silken flowers
Near the garden-cell
carnation and sweet basil
bless the air

Black and white butterflies flit
as mosquitoes whine
but never sting at Compline:
"I have made a pact with them"

Like some brocaded heroine
you make verses
and play the lute
At paseo with your brother
always in church with your mother

    "Ay Jesus de mi alma
    Que bien pareces
    Entre flores y Rosas
    Y Olivas Verdes"

    "Jesus of my soul
    How lovely you appear
    Among flowers and Roses
    And the Green Olive trees"

Your family of thirteen
kept genteel by your needlework,
unlike the Indians and slaves
who, with church bells
and bougainvillea,
populate your city

You nurse them in the room
you pay your parents for,
infirmary for the hidden poor,
those maiden aunts
and women servants used as slaves,
you their girlish herbalist
relying on the mediquito
who sometimes makes a miracle

>   *Ay Jesus de mi alma*
>   *Que bien pareces*
>   *Entre flores y los pobres*
>   *Y Olivas Verdes*

>   Jesus of my soul
>   How lovely you appear
>   Among flowers and the poor
>   And the Green Olive trees

"Like a lioness" between the pirates and the altar
the populace remembers you
but could not know
how you worked at the pieces of solitude

as though with your needle
patterning them into a whole
more brilliant than your birds

While the black-winged Inquisitors
swooped at your song
long enough to bless you
as unlearned
        "What is God like?
        Like ocean infinite
        or like infinite cloud"
and therefore not dangerous

You omitted telling them your vision
of Jesus sitting on two rainbows
with angels and balances
he seemed to doubt:
"After works
comes grace," He said,
"This is the scale of heaven,
and there is none other"

    Jesus of my soul
    How lovely you appear
    Among flowers and Roses
    And the verdant people

    Ay Jesus de mi alma
    Que bien pareces
    Entre flores y Rosas
    Y los pueblos verdes

Dorothy Day

(1897-1980)

D orothy Day grew up in Chicago where she was baptized in the Episcopal Church but fascinated by the piety of the poor. The faith she finally embraced was a social idealism that would address poverty by working to change the world. After two years at college, she moved to New York to work as a reporter for several socialist publications. There she associated with anarchists and artists, among them playwright Eugene O'Neill. When she left her bohemian friends for training as a nurse, she had an affair that led to an abortion.

During World War I, Day joined the suffragist protests in Washington, D.C., and spent thirty days in prison, participating in a hunger strike because of prison conditions. In solitary confinement, she began to read the Bible. A few years later, living with her agnostic lover on Staten

Island, she bore their child. Despite her reservations about the Church, with its "plenty of charity, but too little justice," Day's having a child led her to become a Catholic and end the relationship with the man she loved. She had come to the place where "I wanted to love my enemy, whether capitalist or communist."

In 1932, Day covered the Hunger March of the Unemployed in Washington as a journalist. There she was moved to pray that she might use her talents for workers and the poor. Back in New York, Peter Maurin, a French peasant with an idea, was waiting for her. Together they began *The Catholic Worker* newspaper and houses of hospitality that continue until today and have multiplied. Catholic Workers, like Day and Maurin, are non-violent activists who struggle against systemic violence—what Day called "the dirty rotten system"—and feed and house its victims. They do the works of mercy and justice, aiming to reconstruct a world where it is easier to be good.

In the last thirty years of her life, Day traveled in the U.S. and throughout the world on behalf of justice and peace. With other Catholic leaders, she fasted for a peace statement at Vatican Council II in Rome, and she was arrested with Cesar Chavez in California. In her final years, she declined to travel, saying, "My job now is prayer." Although she invoked the words of Kiriloff in Dostoevsky's *The Possessed*, "All my life I have been haunted by God," she declined to be called a saint because she thought that the title discouraged ordinary people from striving for goodness.

Dorothy Day wrote a moving autobiography, *The Long Loneliness*. Her other works include *On Pilgrimage, Loaves and Fishes*, and several collections of her columns from *The Catholic Worker*. Her final pieces were about God's kindness, nature's beauty, and the need for more mercy and joy in the world.

A child catching crabs on the beach
and fishing for eels in the creek, I felt
      my heart leap up
      at "the name of God,"
but religion was a second hand dress
worn by poor neighbors and maids who knelt
in kitchens nightly, as antidote to the dark,
      the universe spinning
      like a top on a grave.

Through the prison van's gray glass, like the blind
man whose miracle was gradual,
      I made out trees,
      one branch, then another.
In jail our only blanket was darkness
as protestors and prostitutes (I named
with both) spelled each other for sleep,
      outside life lost
      to all but blank prayer.

To New York I came, to its "long loneliness"
and tenement "smells of the grave," to my friends
      never wanting to sleep,
      never wanting to be alone.
I escaped them to nurse the civic poor.
When a son brought lilacs and violets,
I thrilled to pass his mother's bed,
      "life and death
      were so close there."

Desiring abundant life for all,
I nearly found it for myself:
        a lover, our child,
        the ocean spilling fruits
for driftwood fires, lobster and clam juice lunches,
specimens for our window sills, all
the fullness but One who wrenched me from
        my deep and narrow love
        into a wry rebirth.

Empty I came to the church of the poor
that too much regarded the rich,
        cold with charity
        and "little justice."
Thousand of pairs of socks later, and cups
of coffee, community and picket lines,
I know the "swift indifference of the clergy,"
        like a ritual kiss
        morning and night.

If the perfunctory prayer of the priest
only occasionally flames against
        the usual passion
        leveling "gray men,
the color of lifeless trees" in winter squares,
I can embrace "the duty of delight,"
can choose to shelter one small skiff of joy
        in the dark harbor
        of death's battleships.

The Way

Follow the path out of the cave
a straight path after the turn
to light at the open door

or break through the roof of the house
with battering ram a word
Word both passing and divine

Do I speak? I am spoken by
am syllable in God's song
"yes and no and yes again"

in the song that must move on
to dance in light (but I am not
the dancer), to spin in fire

Why not become the fire
that kindles the leaping spark?
Why not the cup that never

empties, well that won't run dry?
Why not the bread like manna
light as Cassian's feather

floating up to God, but plucked
from the hen who gathers chicks
on the porch of Paradise?

No foe this mother God
body broken in childbirth
who holds her breast to us

God who is never late
God who is never early
comes like sun through cloud

flees like the moon at dawn
always and only a friend
issuing invitation:

seek the wild roses by the stream
flowers flanked by thorns,
not flee the sober drunkenness

that reels the stars about the One
We need the night to show us
stars, the "no-ing" dark to trust

If you have understood, it is
not God. Speak in the night
the ninety-nine names of God

When you come to a hundred,
hallow it in silence, the voice
of the other become your voice,

the voice of the world
sighing for horizon
beyond the pain of children.

Break open the cosmic egg,
embrace the lost life,
nothing, costing everything.

"Imagination is a way of doing theology"
   Enduring Grace Flenders

"John on the Cross" -
 - God as shelter - (sheltering mother Hen)
        - The Little Prince -